EXTREME CAREERS

WILDLIFE PHOTOGRAPHERS

Life Through a Lens

Michael A. Sommers

the rosen publishing group's
rosen
central

To Heids Ellison

Published in 2003 by The Rosen Publishing Group, Inc.
29 East 21st Street, New York, NY 10010

Library of Congress Cataloging-in-Publication Data

Sommers, Michael A.
Wildlife photographers : life through a lens / Michael A.
Sommers.—1st ed.
   p. cm. — (Extreme careers)
Includes bibliographical references and index.
ISBN 0-8239-3638-4
1. Wildlife photography—Vocational guidance—Juvenile literature.
[1. Photography of animals. 2. Photography of animals—Vocational
guidance. 3. Vocational guidance.] I. Title. II. Series.
TR729.W54 S66 2003
778.9'32—dc21

2001006684

Manufactured in the United States of America

Contents

A Life of Adventure

Our team was awakened at 4 AM, and at 4:30 we were back on the trail. Actually, "trail" is not really the right way to describe the passage that our local Pygmy guides hacked through the dense brush. Along with the local guides and trackers, our team consisted of a wildlife conservationist, a photographic assistant, and me: the wildlife photographer.

Together, the eight of us had been trekking through the central African jungle for almost four weeks. Our mission: to capture on film some of the rarest wildlife on the face of the earth. It was thrilling to know that we were advancing through unspoiled, beautiful regions in which no human *had ever walked before. However, the stifling heat and humidity, the 200 pounds of supplies and camera gear strapped to our backs, the fear of stepping on a poisonous snake or running into a group of dangerous guerrilla soldiers, and the nasty insects made for tough going. Even with long sleeves and protective headgear with nets, we each ended up with an average of thirty killer-bee stings a day. And the leeches couldn't get enough of us. They stuck to our toes, climbed up our legs, even wormed their way into our sandals.*

By 5 AM, dawn had come and the jungle was alive with strange bird and animal sounds. We had been walking for about two miles, when suddenly, we came to the edge of a clearing. Breathless, we stopped. There, in the early morning mist, was a female gorilla, quietly feeding with her young. We moved forward gingerly. Knowing that few things are more unpredictable than a mother gorilla who feels threatened, our Pygmy guides stayed hidden in the brush.

Slowly, my assistant and I edged closer toward the mother as she worked her way through a salad of plant stems. Luckily, we were downwind and couldn't be detected by the gorilla's sense of smell. As I inched closer, I could see the gorilla up close through my zoom lens. The hair on her head was bright red, and her large, dark eyes were liquid beneath her heavy brows.

Excited by this rare opportunity, I crept closer until my foot snapped a dry twig. Immediately, the gorilla looked up and took two steps in my direction. I froze, paralyzed with excitement and fear. Looking through my lens, her eye seemed to be staring straight into mine. Her gaze was intense and almost human. She looked confused, nervous, and angry all at once. Then, slowly, she returned to her offspring and resumed eating.

During those brief moments, I didn't dare move a muscle except to shoot an entire roll of film. While shooting, I could feel a tsetse fly—a known carrier of fatal tropical diseases—sucking blood from my foot.

—Peter Highman

Professional wildlife photographers live for the rare, often risky, but magical moments like this.

Photographer George Robbins takes pictures of a bobcat rented from Animals of Montana, a company that provides captive-born animals for magazine shoots, commercials, and documentaries.

However, because the earth's last wilderness regions are gradually being invaded by humans, and in spite of technological advances in photographic equipment—more powerful lenses and digital cameras—such moments are increasingly difficult to find. The skill, instinct, courage, and "cool" needed to capture these rare moments on film are what make successful wildlife photography so challenging, dangerous, and exciting.

The First Click

When someone asks you what you want to be when you grow up and you answer, "A wildlife photographer," you might as well have replied that you want to be a rock star or a supermodel. After all, who wouldn't want to get paid to travel around the world taking pictures of white rhinos, red pandas, and other exotic creatures? It's no surprise that wildlife photography is a competitive business that's tough to break into and difficult to make a living from.

Profile of a Wildlife Photographer

There is no clear-cut path to follow for those who dream of becoming wildlife photographers. Perhaps

A diving photographer gets an up-close shot of a green sea turtle in the waters off the Kona coast in Hawaii.

what matters most is the ambition and desire to make your dream a reality. Most wildlife photographers succeed because of their long-held passion for animals and images, their desire to travel and seek out largely unexplored and unpopulated lands, and their love of taking risks.

Many photographers remember the first time they picked up a camera—usually by chance—and began clicking away. Often, their first photos were nothing to write home about. Regardless, these amateurs were

Wildlife Photographers: Life Through a Lens

hooked by the surprising details of the natural world that revealed themselves through their lenses. Once they started shooting, they rarely stopped. And this is the most important rule of becoming a good photographer: Shoot as much film as you can, whenever you can, wherever you are. The most successful photographers take photos every day of their lives.

Aside from taking pictures all the time, a key part of developing one's own style as a photographer is studying the work of others. Pictured here is a room in the Institute of Contemporary Art in Boston, Massachusetts, where many visitors find inspiration.

Any Background Will Do

Today's most successful wildlife photographers come from a variety of backgrounds. Many have college or university degrees, but in subjects ranging from anthropology and environmental and natural sciences to journalism and fine arts. Interestingly, few actually major in photography, although many participate in courses or workshops. According to many photographers, the best education (aside from constantly taking photos) is studying the work of other photographers. A novice or beginner photographer will choose one or several photographers whose work inspires him or her and then try to imitate aspects of the experts' techniques and styles. Often, inspiration also comes from paintings, drawings, and films.

Like other kinds of photography, wildlife photography is more than having technical know-how and the right camera. What gives photographers an individual "signature" or recognizable style are the creative decisions that they make. These can include framing, composition (the organization of elements in the picture), angle, lighting, use of color, and depth of field (how clear or

Wildlife Photographers: Life Through a Lens

blurred the background around the subject is). Think of giraffes, for example, and of how many pictures of giraffes already exist in the world. A successful wildlife photographer must find a giraffe and take its picture in a way that is exciting and original enough to attract attention. Ultimately, what makes a great photographer is not training, technique, or determination, but having an "eye." Having a good eye means having a unique vision, or the ability to see your subject in a creative way that is specific to you.

These giraffes seem curious about the wildlife photographer who is getting a very candid shot of them in this photo. The best photographers capture images of wildlife that are interesting and original.

Getting Started

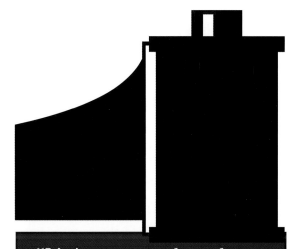

It's unlikely that any photographer will be lucky enough to open up a newspaper and see an advertisement looking for a wildlife photographer—no matter how good or experienced he or she might be. Even very successful professionals have to constantly hustle, making new contacts to whom they can sell their photos and the original stories that accompany them. Wildlife photography is a tough and unpredictable business, especially for those just starting out. Often, photographers spend

"It's important to learn how to make good shots and how to put yourself in situations where you can make great shots. The photographers I most admire are not only technically good, but they can think. They think creatively about how to approach a story, how best to tell a story, and when, where, and how good pictures might happen. Sometimes a good shot happens by intuition, but other times it takes good planning—knowing where to be and when."

—Photographer Chris Anderson, in an interview with NationalGeographic.com years working "day jobs" before they can even make a living from professional photography.

The best way for aspiring photographers to get their foot in the door is by landing a job in which they have access to photographers, editors, or other people in the field. Such people can provide helpful criticisms of their work and are valuable for networking. Some successful photographers began working as journalists or photographers at local newspapers. Others began as photographers' assistants or by doing internships at magazines. Most say that the key to making it is persistence.

A Photographer's Dream Becomes a Reality

Joel Sartore dreamed of being a wildlife photographer. Although he submitted his pictures to *National Geographic*, along with a personal recommendation from one of the famous magazine's top photographers, at first he had no success. He continued sending photos to the magazine every three months. After two years of doing this, Sartore's determination finally paid off: He received a one-day assignment. A few months later, he received a nine-day assignment. Since his first

Many wildlife photographers gain experience and/or find
their calling while taking pictures of subjects that have nothing
to do with nature, such as this fashion photographer doing a
shoot outside of Las Vegas.

assignment in 1990, Sartore has done fourteen features for the magazine. At the same time, he has seen his photos published in many other magazines, such as *Audubon*, *Newsweek*, and *Time*, as well as in books. "Being very type-A, obsessive-compulsive helped me a great deal in getting the *Geographic* to notice me," admits Sartore. "But, be careful . . . There is a fine line between eager and enthusiastic and just being a pain."

A Career on the Edge

Like most photographers these days, the majority of wildlife photographers work as freelancers. This means they sell their services on a per-project basis. Usually, a freelance photographer will approach a magazine with an idea for a story. To come up with an idea usually involves a fair amount of research. If the photographer is planning on doing a piece on hummingbirds in Brazil, for example, he or she will need to know all about hummingbirds and their habitat, as well as how, when, and where to photograph them. Often, a photographer will do research at a site beforehand.

A photographer in a safari vehicle takes pictures of the breathtaking wilderness of Tanzania.

The Hook

Research will also help the photographer discover a good "hook." A hook is a specific angle that helps shape the story and give it a focus. For example, taking pictures of a bunch of hummingbirds zooming around pretty tropical flowers does not make for an original story. Most people have seen hummingbird photographs a hundred times before. A possible hook would be to focus on the scores of hummingbirds in Brazilian cities that come to feed at the windows of houses and apartment buildings. Only, instead of sucking nectar from flowers, they drink the sugar and water mixture that people put in hummingbird feeders. The result—that many of these birds are suffering from diabetes and even obesity because they are eating too much sugar— makes for an original story.

The Budget

If a story is approved, the photographer will meet with a magazine's illustration or photo editor to plan out and organize how the assignment will proceed. A budget will be calculated that estimates the cost of the shoot. The budget must be approved by the editor of the magazine.

Being on Assignment

Freelance photographers often work on one or more projects at the same time. They also work for more than one client. It is not uncommon for one photographer to work for various magazines in different countries, while contributing to books, shooting advertising campaigns, taking photos for a Web site or CD-ROM, or even filming a wildlife documentary on video. A photographer can be off shooting penguins in Antarctica for four months and then be without work for six months. Being on assignment means living an adventurous lifestyle in which you are literally living out of a knapsack, often in extreme conditions. As Joel Sartore points out, "Being a freelance photojournalist in general is not for the faint of heart; it's feast or famine—definitely not a steady job."

Some of the Options

When an editor or other client is repeatedly pleased with a freelancer's work, he or she might begin to

A photographer closes in on some birds resting below him on a cliff in the Pribilof Islands in Alaska.

contract the photographer when in need of photos for a specific story or assignment. At this point, the photographer becomes a contract photographer. Magazines that have their own in-house staff photographer are becoming increasingly rare. A staff photographer works full-time for a publication and is responsible for taking pictures on a permanent basis.

Preparing the Shoot

W ith the go-ahead to shoot a story, a photographer has to do some careful planning. This may include talking to natural scientists and conservationists who study the wildlife and natural habitat in which the shoot is to take place. This kind of research helps the photographer understand the habits and behavior of his or her subjects, as well as any other animals that may share or live near the habitat.

Scouting a Location

It is also important to consult books or experts who know as much as possible about the natural

Original photos often contain elements that are not normally found together, which makes the photo interesting and unique, such as this one of a giraffe and man running together in Kenya.

environment. This not only helps the photographer decide when to shoot (avoiding hurricane or brushfire season, for example) but also to be on guard for dangers that could range from flooded rivers and avalanches to poisonous spiders, armed poachers, and fatal diseases. Often, the only way to choose, or scout, a location is to travel to the region.

On-site, you can stake out the best places for spotting animals and taking photos, and talk firsthand with specialists and knowledgeable locals. Scouting a location can take weeks or even months. But it is essential for determining what equipment, supplies, and assistants will be needed; what approaches to take in shooting a specific animal; and the duration and cost of a shoot.

When wildlife photographer Michael "Nick" Nichols discovered that *National Geographic* magazine was planning a feature on tigers, he asked the editor to let him go to India for five weeks to try to find some wild tigers to shoot. Because tigers in the wild are extremely hard to catch sight of, let alone photograph, the magazine agreed to let Nichols go right away. In India, Nichols consulted with one of the world's leading tiger scientists from the Wildlife Conservation Society. This specialist told Nichols that his only real chance was to go to a specific wildlife reserve during the dry season. Only there, where the forest's vegetation was less dense, would he have a chance of glimpsing the easily camouflaged tigers. Furthermore, since the reserve was open to tourists, the tigers would be used to humans—in jeeps and on elephants.

During those five weeks, Nichols sighted tigers sixteen times and ended up with one publishable photograph. Locals said Nichols was very lucky. Nichols then convinced the magazine's editor that with more money, more time (seven months), and special permission allowing him to travel through the park on foot, he could complete an entire story. Because it was the dry season and the water supply was low, he knew that if he waited around the reserve's few water holes, he would get his tigers when they emerged from their deep cover for a drink.

Gear and Equipment

It doesn't matter if you're stuck on an island of Antarctic ice or crawling for weeks through a particularly soggy section of the Amazon forest. If you trip and smash your

The amount of equipment wildlife photographers must carry with them can be staggering. Camera equipment alone makes for a heavy load to transport through sometimes hostile natural environments.

camera, if a flood washes your food supply away, or if you realize that you left the snake-bite ointment at the camp, remember, walking two blocks to the nearest corner store is not an option. Although time and technology have made camera equipment and camping supplies lighter, more compact, and portable, the amount of gear a wildlife photographer has to lug around is no laughing matter. Aside from basic food, shelter, all-weather clothing, and medical supplies—all of which need to be carefully wrapped and protected in

To capture the perfect shot, a photographer must at times put himself or herself in danger in order to find new perspectives.

unbreakable, air-proof, and waterproof containers— here are what some of the experts routinely tote around in the wild:

- Seven or more different camera "bodies." After all, if your camera falls in a river, you can't just give up and go home.
- An assortment of lenses, filters, tripods, flashes, and light meters.
- Film, film, and more film (usually Kodak or Fuji slide film). A thousand rolls is a good start.

- Dry, canned, or dehydrated food.
- Scaffolding to build tree "hides" (which are sometimes thirty or forty feet off the ground).
- Knee and elbow pads for those lying-down-on-the-ground-and-waiting shots.

The Team

The various people who make up a photographer's team depend on the length, focus, and level of difficulty of the assignment(s). It also depends on where the shoot is taking place and on the budget. Photographers are usually aided by a photographic assistant and are often accompanied by a specialist, scientist, conservationist, and/or journalist with experience in the field who is responsible for writing the story's text. Local guides, who know the ins and outs and potential dangers of the area, are often necessary. So are animal trackers, who, like some guides, know certain animals' feeding, sleeping, mating, and migrating habits by heart.

Photographers, such as these taking pictures of an elk herd in Wyoming's Yellowstone National Park, often work with assistants, scientists with expertise in the subjects that are being photographed, and local guides who know the area.

Danger on the Blue Nile

Photographer Nevada Wier and writer Virginia Morell followed the Blue Nile to Ethiopia for a *National Geographic* feature. Among the many dangerous situations the two women encountered was the following, narrated by Morell in an interview for *National Geographic*.

"We were approached by men armed with AK-47s. They introduced themselves as officials, but we were suspicious; they looked like a band of brigands. There was a roughness about them, and they were exceedingly hostile to us. They refused to accept any of the permits or letters that allowed us to be there. It was very tense. They tried to force us to go with them into the high mountains so they could wire Addis Ababa, they claimed, to confirm that we were legitimate. Eventually, we had to pay them to make them go away.

"The atmosphere eased tremendously after they left. But we could tell from the looks on their faces that they could have killed us and not thought twice about it."

Being Cautious Pays Off

For long treks in areas with a high risk of disease, a medical specialist might accompany the group. On one assignment, Swedish photographer Mattias Klum almost died from a typhoid-salmonella infection. Because of this previous experience, and since most of his team would not be accustomed to the local diet and cuisine, Klum decided to bring along a tropical disease specialist while photographing lions in Asia. It was a smart move, and nobody experienced anything worse than an upset stomach and diarrhea—with one unfortunate exception: the specialist himself, who became extremely sick and didn't recover for months.

In regions where there is a risk of coming into contact with hostile humans, an armed security guard is sometimes necessary. When photographer Chris Anderson went on assignment to the Central African Republic, his team hired Raymond Yakoro, an officer in the national army's special forces unit. To protect the group from poachers and wildlife, Yakoro carried an AK-47 rifle at all times.

Eye-to-Eye with the Animals

Most wild animals are not what you would call willing models. While few actually go out of their way to attack humans—unless they are threatened or very, very hungry—most hide or run away at the first sound, scent, or glimpse of a human being. Because of this, it is often very difficult to find a wild model, let alone take a picture of one.

Tracking Models in the Wild

Often, photographers require the help of a guide, tracker, or wildlife specialist familiar with an animal's behavior, habits, and environment. It is equally important for photographers to have a lot of patience, combined with an understanding of and respect for their wild models.

As we saw before, photographer Nick Nichols had a really difficult time tracking tigers. After all, a tiger is a predator whose whole life is based on not being seen so it can sneak up on its prey. For Nichols and his assistant, an average day began with them entering the tiger reserve before dawn (around 5 AM). They rode elephants while guides went ahead in a jeep looking for tiger tracks. By 8 AM, if no tracks were found, there was probably no chance of finding a tiger for the rest of the day. If they did come across tracks, Nichols would follow them on his elephant.

While following the trail, Nichols would listen for alarm calls. He had discovered that birds, monkeys, and deer all make warning noises whenever a tiger is around. After a while, he could even tell from the type of noise whether the tiger was walking or lying down, coming or going. Whenever he heard an urgent alarm call, Nichols would ride over and sometimes find the tiger. Frequently, however, "finding" a tiger meant catching a quick glimpse of one. Eventually, Nichols resorted to two techniques that are very common in wildlife photography: hides and camera traps.

Hides

A hide is a simple hut, usually made of grass and branches that "hide" the photographer while he or she waits to photograph an animal (at the animal's home, watering hole, or feeding ground, for example). The difficult part is being very silent and not moving a muscle for long periods of time.

When Mattias Klum spent fourteen months in the jungles of Malaysia, he built his hides—also called "blinds"—on platforms, some of which were over 200 feet high. Knowing which food certain animals liked, he placed the platforms in trees with ripening fruit. Klum calculated his position so that he would have a perfect view of animals feeding. Then he waited for weeks and months for the right light and for shy animals to appear. While waiting, Klum and his team were soaked by torrential rains and attacked by bloodsucking leeches. But the animals came.

Camera Traps

When a photographer sets up a camera so that it will automatically take pictures of an animal on its own,

This photographer on Sanibel Island, Florida, uses a clump of bushes as a hide in order to photograph his subjects without scaring them away.

this is known as a camera trap. The camera is attached to highly sensitive electronic equipment that is programmed to react to either motion or sound. When an animal is in the camera's range, an infrared beam detects its movement or noise and triggers the camera's shutter.

Although it sounds simple, it takes a lot of careful calculation to construct a trap. The photographer has to choose a good spot, such as a feeding area, and then estimate where exactly the animal will pass and at what time. Angles, lighting, and background need to be carefully measured and judged. Changes in light throughout the day and the speed at which the animal is moving all have to be taken into account. Lenses and flashes (for night photography) also need to be carefully selected.

Often, a photographer will set up various camera traps throughout an area and then check on them every few days. Photos taken in this manner can yield fantastic results because they capture an animal in private, without the instrusion of a human being. Another benefit of this is that the animals can be photographed in places where no sane photographer would go—the den of a ten-foot-long Komodo dragon, for example.

Some people claim that with camera traps it's the camera, and not the photographer, taking the picture. However, it's the photographer who chooses the lighting, framing, and background, and who makes the other creative decisions that ultimately make the images his or hers.

Getting Close

Although hides and camera traps are two ways of getting good shots, using a hide means sitting in the same place for long periods of time, while camera traps involve a lot of film, luck, and trial and error. Because photographers can't always wait for animals to come to them, they often have to go to the animals. One way of doing this is to do as animals themselves do—resort to camouflage. A great way of blending in is to travel on the back of another animal, such as a horse or, better yet, an elephant. Most animals won't view the photographer as a human but as just part of another beast (albeit a strange looking one). In this way, photographers can get very close to their models. Elephants often double as ideal vehicles

Crouching low on a rocky slope on Mount Evans in Colorado, a photographer captures a small herd of bighorn sheep on film.

since they can navigate rough terrain better than even the toughest jeep and are basically fearless—even of lions, tigers, and cheetahs. On the downside, they can be very slow, and their bumpy movements make it very difficult to focus and shoot.

Up Close and Personal

Some wildlife photographers get close to animals by immersing themselves in their subjects' lives. Dutch wildlife photographer Frans Lanting spends enormous amounts of time getting close to his models. He observes them, mimics them, and lives with them, gaining their trust until he becomes accepted as one of the group. Frequently, he ends up establishing relationships with individual animals. Becoming part of a pride of lions meant that when the group went to feed on a freshly killed gazelle, Lanting was "invited" to tag along and photograph the banquet at close range.

For another project, Lanting lived among elephant seals off the coast of California. To understand what it must be like to be an elephant seal, and how to move like one, he imagined that he was living in a sleeping bag filled with jello. This wasn't just for fun but for survival. Adult elephant seals can weigh up to three tons. When they feel threatened—usually by any creature that uses different body language—they become extremely aggressive. Living (carefully) among them, Lanting witnessed horrible fights between males that resulted in torn-up trunks, bloody wounds, and chunks of flesh left floating in the sea. In spite of the risk, these unbelievable experiences are part of the thrill of the job.

Complications with Elephants

As he relates in his book *Handful of Tiger Time*, when scouting tigers in India, Nick Nichols broke three cameras that fell off the lurching elephant he was riding. For his second try, he brought along a specially padded chair for his back. He also took a bottle to urinate in. The first time he had tried to relieve himself while on the elephant, the Indian guide had yelled at him: "This is God. You can't stand up and pee off God!" The guide then explained that in India the much-loved god Ganesh appears in the form of an elephant.

Taking pictures from a raft, these photographers take advantage of a walrus's naturally poor eyesight to get a closer shot of the animal. Being downwind also helps them elude the walrus's sense of smell.

Too Close for Comfort

When dealing with wild animals, there's getting close and there's getting too close. Sometimes, it's hard to know where the boundary lies. But responsible photographers always consider the welfare of their subjects. Part of the excitement and danger of photographing wild animals is the degree of unpredictability that exists in this type of work. After all, because they are wild, you never know exactly what animals will do or how they will react. In addition, there is always an element of risk taking involved. Sometimes this can result in a fantastic photo, but it can also result in a near-death experience.

Magic Moments

As we have seen, being a successful wildlife photographer depends on many things. It depends on good planning, a firm knowledge of animals and their environments, a good eye, creativity, and

An intrepid photographer got this closeup shot of tiger cubs despite the danger involved in arousing the anger of their mother, who is certainly close by.

Danger Zone

"You want to get the shot, but . . . sometimes you go too far," confesses Nick Nichols in an article in *National Geographic*, describing how he approached a female tiger's den to take some pictures. "We weren't trying to disturb her, and we were trying to maintain a safe distance. We felt we were doing something that was ethically OK. We knew there were boundaries.

"We stumbled right onto the den, with the cubs in it," Nichols goes on. "We didn't have any weapons. The tigress charged. Despite the fact that you're told ad nauseam never to run if attacked, we ran. I was trampled by the two [guides]! I was running, don't get me wrong, but they were running faster and they ran over me. I fractured my jaw and scraped my leg on the rocks. I was completely in shock. I felt tremendous guilt toward myself and all of us for being there. If she had killed us, she would have been shot dead."

Wildlife Photographers: Life Through a Lens

familiarity with camera techniques. Patience, courage, physical and emotional endurance, and risk taking are involved. So are two final factors: luck and good instincts.

Looking Up at a Deadly Snake

Wildlife photographer Darlyne A. Murawski had a magic if scary moment when on assignment in Ecuador, which she recounted on NationalGeographic.com:

"I saw three giant anacondas at the Cuyabeno Reserve in Ecuador. According to the locals, it's unusual to see so many in such a short time. One male snake was about sixteen feet [five meters] long, and the two females were about twenty-five feet [eight meters] long . . . We spotted one of the female snakes perched on a limb jutting out of a lagoon. We were passing in a long dugout canoe, so we stopped to photograph it. Then the boat drifted underneath it. It gave me the creeps! I was worried that this 400-pound [180-kilogram] snake would fall down on me and do something horrible."

Although every photographer hopes for some luck, none can depend upon it. Good instincts mean that no matter how much planning photographers do ahead of time, when circumstances change (and they will), the photographer knows how to improvise and take advantage of them. Similarly, when an unexpected opportunity occurs, the photographer is ready to capture it on film. Often, it is this combination of luck and instinct that leads to magic moments.

Back from the Wilderness

For an average magazine article, wildlife photographers might spend between four weeks and four months in the field. Often, they make several trips during different seasons. It is not uncommon for photographers to shoot anywhere from 400 to over 1,000 rolls of film (generally thirty-six exposures each) for large features. Thirty thousand pictures may seem like a lot, but most photographers start off "sketching" with their cameras. They undertake a visual exploration of their subjects by shooting them in many different ways. This experimentation often leads to original and surprising images.

So Much Film, So Few Pictures

During the time photographers are in the field, they are constantly sending back film to the magazine's illustration or photo editor. Often, a photographer will send the film in various shipments in order to guard against the loss of or damage to some rolls. After each shipment has been processed and edited, the photographer contacts the editor and discusses the photos. Together, they decide how the assignment is going: what images work, what images are missing, and so on.

At a certain point, the photographer might come to the magazine and work with the editor to select the best photos before returning to the field. Other staff members are often involved in these creative decisions, such as art directors and designers, who are responsible for the article's layout. (Layout refers to the way images and text are creatively assembled on a page.) When the assignment is finished, the photographer is often involved in the final process of choosing and editing the photos. Once the magazine's editor has

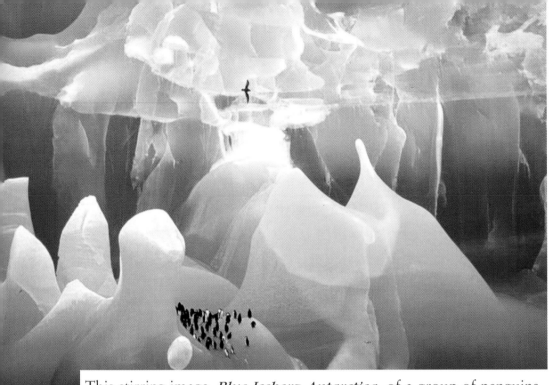

This stirring image, *Blue Iceberg, Antarctica*, of a group of penguins on a rarely seen blue iceberg, won the photographer, Cherry Alexander, the Natural History Museum's Wildlife Photographer of the Year Award in October 1995.

approved the images, they are laid out as they will appear in the published magazine.

The Impact of a Photo

You have probably heard the expression "A picture is worth a thousand words." This saying rings particularly true when it comes to wildlife photography. Even fifteen or twenty years ago, wildlife photography was often viewed as a fun career where images of cute or exotic animals amazed and entertained the public. Today, the alarming rate of the destruction of the earth's wilderness has increased environmental awareness and has made saving our ecosystems—and the animals that inhabit them—one of the world's most important challenges. If you imagine that photos published by *National Geographic* alone are viewed by between 30 and 40 million people around the world, you can begin to see what an impact one photo can have.

Wildlife Photography and Environmentalism

It is not surprising that almost all wildlife photographers are also strong environmentalists. They often view themselves as privileged links between the increasingly endangered creatures of the wild and the well-meaning but ignorant humans with whom they share the planet. A photo of a mother cheetah nursing her cubs or a shot of a rare flying squirrel gives the problem of endangerment and extinction an identifiable face.

Wildlife Photographers: Life Through a Lens

Images of animals in the wild can lead to many positive changes. They can influence the adoption of environmental laws and policies, and

Making an Impact

In 1990, *National Geographic* published Frans Lanting's wildlife photographs from the Okavango Delta in the African nation of Botswana, best known for diamond mining. After the magazine came out, the Botswana Embassy in Washington, D.C., was bombarded with phone calls from Americans asking for information about tours or the possibilities of starting businesses there. The publicity also led Botswana's government to create new policies that would ensure the region's conservation. "Such publicity is needed at this critical moment in history," explains Lanting on his Web site, http://www.lanting.com. "Botswana's government . . . is only beginning to understand the natural treasures they possess—in the long run, perhaps, a lot more valuable than their diamonds."

spur the creation of wildlife reserves and sanctuaries. They can also lead to the protection of certain species and to the conviction of those who threaten them, such as land developers, hunters, and poachers.

Expanding Roles

While the study and preservation of wildlife has become increasingly important, so has the role of the

Many wildlife photographers, such as James Balog, pictured here with a Sumatran orangutan and fifteen images of stamps he unveiled in 1995, have worked to preserve endangered species through their work.

Wildlife Photographers: Life Through a Lens

wildlife photographer. Today's wildlife photographers do far more than just take pictures for books and magazines. Many participate in or even begin their own wildlife conservation projects, which aim to save the animals they photograph as well as educate

Two photographers film a curious polar bear in Wapusk, Manitoba, during a shoot in the Canadian wilderness.

the public. Their images are found in documentary and feature films, tourist brochures and advertising campaigns, environmental reports and scientific pamphlets, calendars and greeting cards, and Web sites and e-zines. Many photographers have also gone online. Images shot with digital cameras can be downloaded directly onto a computer, where they are then edited. Photographers can also set up their own online catalogs through which they can sell their images to anyone who happens to surf by. Ultimately though, more important than technology is what takes place in the wilderness itself.

When Joel Sartore went to the rain forests of Bolivia, it took him ten days to get a publishable photo of a macaw. A shot of a jaguar took months of preparation with local guides. While waiting for these perfect shots, he dodged killer pigs, slept with bats and sweat bees (an African bee), and eased the boredom by digging maggots out of his skin. "So why do it?" the photographer asks himself before answering his own question on his Web site, http://www.joelsartore.com. "[Because] the rewards are just as extreme as the work. How often does a person get a chance to save a rain forest?"

Glossary

Addis Ababa The capital city of Ethiopia.

blind A simple lean-to or hut made of grass and branches that hides a wildlife photographer from animals.

brigand A bandit.

budget The amount of money reserved for a certain purpose.

camera trap A camera that is set up to automatically photograph an animal.

composition Organization of elements included in a photograph.

depth of field The clarity or blurriness of the background in a photograph.

framing The composition of elements around the subject of a photo that provides a natural frame.

freelance To work independently on a per-project basis.

habitat A creature's home or living environment.

hide Same as a blind.

hook The specific angle or focus of a story.

layout The design or arrangement of text and photographs to be printed.

light meter A small instrument that measures the amount of available light.

nomadic To roam from place to place without a permanent home.

salmonella A poisonous bacteria.

scaffolding A temporary, above-ground platform constructed for shooting from heights.

scout To search for a location that suits one's needs.

tracker A person who follows animals' tracks or traces.

tripod A three-legged camera stand.

type A An aggressive, impatient, competitive type of personality.

water hole A natural hole containing water that animals use to drink or bathe in.

wildlife conservationist One who protects the existence of creatures in the wild.

zoom lens A camera lens that makes a subject appear closer or farther away.

For More Information

Moose Peterson's Wildlife Research Photography
P.O. Box 3628
Mammoth Lakes, CA 93546-3628
(760) 924-8632
Web site: http://www.moose395.net

National Audubon Society
700 Broadway
New York, NY 10003
(212) 979-3000
Web site: http://www.audubon.org

National Geographic Society
1145 17th Street NW
Washington, DC 20036-4688
(800) NGS-LINE (647-5463)
Web site: http://www.nationalgeographic.com

For More Information

National Wildlife Federation
11100 Wildlife Center Drive
Reston, VA 20190-5362
(703) 438-6000
Web site: http://www.nwf.org

Photo Traveler
P.O. Box 39912
Los Angeles, CA 90039
(800) 417-4680
(323) 660-8600
Web site: http://www.phototravel.com

Wildlife Conservation Society
2300 Southern Boulevard
Bronx, NY 10460
(718) 220-5100
Web site: http://www.wcs.org

World Wildlife Fund
1250 24th Street NW
Washington, DC 20037
(800) CALL-WWF (225-5993)
(202) 293-4800
Web site: http://www.worldwildlife.org

Magazines

Adventure
Audubon
International Wildlife
National Geographic
National Geographic for Kids
National Wildlife
Outdoor Photographer
Popular Photography
Ranger Rick
Wildlife Conservation
World Magazine

Web Sites

Due to the changing nature of Internet links, the Rosen Publishing Group, Inc., has developed an online list of Web sites related to the subject of this book. This site is updated regularly. Please use this link to access the list:

http://www.rosenlinks.com/eca/wiph/

For Further Reading

Aaseng, Nathan. *Wildshots: The World of the Wildlife Photographer*. Brookfield, CT: Millbrook Press, 2001.

Burian, Peter K., and Robert Caputo. *National Geographic Photography Field Guide*. Washington, DC: National Geographic Society, 1999.

Klum, Mattias. *Borneo Rainforest*. San Francisco: Chronicle Books, 1998.

McDonald, Joe. *The New Complete Guide to Wildlife Photography*. New York: Watson-Guptill Publications, 1998.

Peterson, Moose. *Wildlife Photography: Getting Started in the Field*. Rochester, NY: Tiffen Company, 1997.

Taylor Young, Mary. *On the Trail of Colorado Critters: Wildlife Watching for Kids*. Englewood, CO: Westcliffe Publishing, 2000.

Bibliography

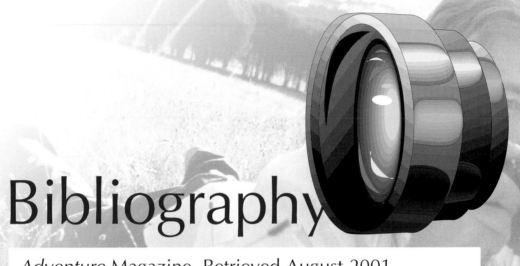

Adventure Magazine. Retrieved August 2001
(http://www.nationalgeographic.com/adventure).

Bob Atkins Photography. Retrieved August 2001
(http://bobatkins.photo.net).

Fordyce, Graeme. "Running With Wolves." *Outdoor Photographer*, September 1999.

Frans Lanting Online. Retrieved August 2001
(http://www.lanting.com).

Harris, Mark Edward. "Secret Worlds of Nature."
Outdoor Photographer, June 2001.

Joel Sartore Photography. Retrieved August 2001
(http://www.joelsartore.com).

John Shaw Photography. Retrieved August 2001
(http://www.johnshawphoto.com).

Klum Photography. Retrieved August 2001 (http://www.klumphotography.com).

Lawrence, James. "Art of the Jungle." *Outdoor Photographer*, January 2001.

Natalie Fobes Photography. Retrieved August 2001 (http://www.fobesphoto.com).

National Geographic Magazine. Retrieved August 2001 (http://www.nationalgeographic.com).

National Geographic Photographer Biographies. Retrieved August 2001 (http://www.nationalgeographic.com/photography/biographies/index.html).

National Geographic's Photography Page. Retrieved August 2001 (http://www.nationalgeographic.com/photography).

Nichols, Nick. *A Handful of Tiger Time*. Published in 1997. Retrieved August 2001 (http://www.nationalgeographic.com/nichols/f_assignment.html).

Sunrise Photography: A Photographer's Resource. Retrieved August 2001 (http://www.sunrisephoto.net).

Werner, Steven. "Tiger Beat." *Outdoor Photographer*. December 1998.

Index

Index

About the Author

Michael A. Sommers is a freelance journalist who has a twin sister. He has written numerous books for young readers.

Photo Credits

Cover, pp. 17, 29, 35, 52 © Index Stock; pp. 7, 48, 51 © AP/World Wide Photos; pp. 9, 10, 12, 15, 20, 23, 26, 27, 38, 41, 42 © Corbis.

Design

Les Kanturek

Layout

Nelson Sá